Of Dirt and Tar

To Dan
You can nevah
nevah nevah
evah retire —
We're in this
together —
Don't leave!

XOXO
June

Of Dirt and Tar

Poems by June Sylvester Saraceno

Cherry Grove Collections

Published by Cherry Grove Collections
P.O. Box 541106
Cincinnati, OH 45254-1106

ISBN: 9781625490742
LCCN: 2014932721

Poetry Editor: Kevin Walzer
Business Editor: Lori Jareo

Visit us on the web at www.cherry-grove.com

Cover photo by Missa Coffman for Lost Coast Culture Machine
Cover and interior design by Courtney Berti
Author photo by Carolina Cruz Guimarey

Acknowledgements

Grateful acknowledgement goes to the editors of the following journals and anthologies in which these poems, or earlier versions of them, first appeared:

A Bird as Black as the Sun: California Poets on Crows and Ravens: "This Winter"

American Journal of Nursing: "Skin" and "Heart Monitor"

Common Ground: "Where the Girls Are"

Connotation Press: "At a Bazaar"

Fifth Wednesday: "Figures in a Field" and "Directions for Early Morning Departures"

IthacaLit: "Last Beautiful Moment," "After School Lessons," and "Tadpole Lament"

The Kokanee: "Persephone" and "Old Maid Shuffle"

Mead: The Magazine of Literature and Libations: "This is Outside My House"

Moonshine Ink: "December's Shift"

Northwind: "Literary Barbie"

Poetry Quarterly: "Nancy Drew in the Alzheimer's Ward" and "Spinning Dorothy"

Southwestern American Literature: "Mrs. Robinson Takes a Night Class" and "Xantippe Confides in Her Neighbor"

Two Hawks Quarterly: "Skiing the Yard Sale"

Worchester Review: "What Light Brings"

Word Riot: "In a Study of the Meadow"

Heartfelt thanks to my friends and family for love and support along the way. Deep gratitude for advice on this collection of poems goes to Laura McCullough and April Ossmann, and to Courtney Berti for visionary assistance with book design. Grateful respect to the lyricist Robert Hunter whose songs have given me ground for much contemplation over the years, *Box of Rain* in particular. Special appreciation goes to Camac Art Center in France for time and space to write. A big thanks to Sierra Arts Foundation for the writing grant. Finally, my gratitude to Kevin Walzer and Lori Jareo at WordTech Communications.

For Anthony and Dylan, with love times infinity

Table of Contents

I

Ways to Leave Your Body.................................1
The Last Beautiful Moment.................................2
Waiting Room 3
At a Bazaar.................................4
Heart Monitor.................................6
This Winter.................................7
Skiing the Yard Sale.................................8
Proposition.................................9
Ancient Tango.................................10
Drunk Driving.................................11
Bifocals.................................12
Literary Barbie 13
That Way 14

II

One Way.................................19
Shame.................................20
Tadpole Lament.................................21
Skin.................................22
Figures in a Field.................................23
After School Lessons.................................24
Living Near Lucky.................................25
Receptionist at the Family Planning Clinic......26

III

Persephone's Shade.................................31
Spinning Dorothy 33
Xantippe Confides in Her Neighbor.................................34
Catherine the Great.................................35
Nancy Drew in the Alzheimer's Ward.................................36
Prolific.................................37
Mrs. Robinson Takes a Night Class.................................38
Blundering Alice 40
In a Study of the Meadow.................................41

Old Maid Shuffle..42
Where the Girls Are..43

IV

This Inside is My House.......................................47
December's Shift...48
Directions for Early Morning Departures.......49
Bottled..50
Quadrille..51
Doves and Thieves..52
This is Outside My House...................................53
Thou still unravished bride of quiet time........54
Tracing a Distance..56
What Light Brings..57
Meadow Grammar...59

I

Such a long, long time to be gone, and a short time to be there.
Robert Hunter, *Box of Rain*

Ways to Leave Your Body

You think you are in your body
when you're inside your head,
but you could be any place at all.

Move your parts like a doll and watch
from a distance as you lift the hand
in a gesture of farewell or hello.

Leave her placed there just so.
Travel beyond borders of blood and bone.
Strike out for parts unknown.

Open your third eye,
but don't dismiss illusion as illusion.
Nexus of starry-eyed and star.

You may brush by death along the way.
Greetings are not necessary, a nod will do.

Integrate it all—the now, the touch, vision,
balance, pulse, sound, space—bring it all together
and allow it to carry you unanchored away.

Encounter yourself from the outside.
Shake your hand. Say what you need to say
to move on.

The Last Beautiful Moment
for Russell and Elizabeth

Unanchored abruptly into thin air,
she arced toward the sun,
dandelion-head with a backdrop
pooling blue.

In that last beautiful moment,
before the gravity of boulders
and jagged granite teeth,
she was wingless sylph
sky-borne.

He held her aloft in his eye.
His hands in unharnessed time,
drew the fire and air
that delivered her
back to light.

Waiting Room

Four of us are reading glossy magazines
or staring into space, avoiding each other's eyes,
when the old man with a walker creeps in.
In labored slow motion, he lowers himself
into the chair across from me,
eyes the basket of goodies on a low table.

He tries to scoot his chair forward.
It doesn't budge. He leans in, extends a shaky hand
toward the cornucopia between us.
I bend forward, "Can I pass you something?"
His bushy white brows knit over a rheumy glare.
He rumbles an angry *urrrrrrr* sound
as if to ward me off.

I lift the basket towards him.
He claws Rice Krispie treats, granola bars, Fig Newtons
piles them in his lap. He gnaws at the wrappers
until they give way. He eats it all, smacking
and spilling and sometimes even grunting.

We pretend not to watch. We blink,
avert our eyes from his obvious hunger.
At some point in eternity a nurse comes for him.
She waits in the doorway, upright and unmoving,
as he slowly ratchets himself up,
crumbs and cellphone fall around him
a path of shedding skin, debris,
marking his way out.

At a Bazaar

Under speckled light
  scattered from an antler chandelier,
I find strange wonders:
  A miniature Siberia plays Lara's theme.
      It fills me with nostalgia,
  how I wept for Zhivago and his loves.
A blue and white porcelain shoe
  conjures my grandmother.
A yellowed map,
      so brittle I still and hold my breath near it.

At one table, a woman talks to a child at her feet
…just lay down…go to sleep. By the time you wake up,
you'll be home. The girl is curled
      on a faux Persian rug rolled over the cement floor.
      I look at her tangle of brown hair
          and wonder at this simple magic,
              her travel from place to place
                  through the incantation of sleep.
      I wonder if I lie down beside her
which home I would wake in.

I want to keep nothing,
      even though these treasures ease me.
I drift through a boomerang of dust,
  dusk gathers, hum of slow,
      unpremeditated conversations
          droning in this hive.

For months, I've been little other than a zoo of nerves,
  but this makeshift world
      with its bone structure lighting,
          each stall with its own singular beasts of flotsam,
              or history, or revamped trash,
are as soothing as stabled horses

snorting out a soft,
        wet invitation to throw yourself on
            the back of something that breaks from the dark
  into a gallop,
and head out heedless on the path to daylight.

Heart Monitor

Even predictable irritants speed the pulse a little:
The clunking car sound only disappears when the mechanic is near.
The baby wakes up just as you ever-so-gently lie him back in the crib.
Even if you only pour the glass half full, the milk ends up spilled.

There's always more traffic when you're late,
the button pops when you put on your party dress,
a car alarm goes off every other hour the night before the big interview.
And then your children move away and the at-first blessed silence
becomes accursed and your heart races when the phone rings
because you hope for good news bubbling up from their far away voices
and even more strongly you fear the call that signals doom,
but the let down: it's just a robo-call telling you your carpets are dirty.

Along the way, the house where you grew up is torn down.
The leafy streets of childhood, the helpful grocer, the neighbor
who will watch your dog, they melt into oblivion.
Your hands turn into aliens, the snoring that wakes you
must be your own. There's no one there.
One day you're lying in the middle of some unknown—
a person of a certain age grown uncertain
counting up the predictable losses, losing count, starting over.

You feel a flutter in your chest and think is it a muscle or a bird?
It must be muscle, and maybe what held it in place and flexing
was all the needling things that kept it from going soft,
kept it from becoming an atrophied sack
that no longer squeezed and pumped you toward something like life.

This Winter

The crows seem larger than life.
That one there—big as a cow,
sheen of jet feathers, marble-eyed surveyor,
gauges me as I approach.

Maybe it is a shift in proportion
brought on by winter.
My shadow wanes, dulled grey
and somewhat featureless on the frost.
The crow is an inky country by contrast.

This indifferent crow holds his ground.
I consider running madly at him
flapping to startle him into flight.
Then I consider the ditch between us
and continue my slow pace.

Passing, I see something dangles
from his beak—entrails? a dark ribbon?
the shoelace of the last person
who tried to jar him into the sky?

"You win," I mutter under my breath.
A little uneasy at his presence behind me,
outside of my vision, I speed up slightly,
as though moving towards a deadline
that must be met.

Skiing the Yard Sale

Retelling the story, I'm too embarrassed to name
the bunny hill where I lay splayed like a rag doll,
a trail of gear marking the tumble of my undoing.

Endless equations of people dangled on the lift above,
suspended and swaying, their skis forming X's V's
and elevens over my face. My third day on skis,
this view was new to me. Flushed, I considered
my own over-exposed angles, the new geometry of me:
one leg pinned, two arms in awkward slashes against the snow,
taking a beat before heaving up the sum of my parts
to gather what I had lost on the hill above me
—a pole, a ski, hat, sunglasses, another pole, ski...

How lucky it seemed then when someone yelled
"YARD SALE!" above the shushing of upright skiers.
I was grateful for anything that would distract the eyes
from my awkward arrangement on the snow.

Even the amplified laughter and smattering
of applause was not enough to clue me in
that my public unpinning had been heralded on high
just in case anyone might have looked the other way.

Proposition

Look, Sleep, I bring you flowers. Love me.
I'm going to write a sonnet for you. I make time
for you. I need you to return the favor. Only
not when I'm driving. Not during the public address
where the gunfire in my head turns abruptly
into applause, leaves me wondering whether I snored.

It doesn't have to be like this, poorly timed flirtations.
You could meet me between the sheets. I would embrace
your soft erasure, give up my all to your enveloping
demand. Travel gladly with you to exotic expanses
where we slip into splintered beings and elastic time.
Tonight. Come to me. We will traverse the marrow bone.

Ancient Tango

When the man seated by me on the plane yanks his daughter's arm,
I startle from the calm blue zone of almost asleep and feel
a searing red flame, stiletto sharp, slice my center.
He whispers through clenched teeth "stop it, shut up" as she whimpers.
Seething, I tell myself, settle, breathe, but peace recedes,
goes out the window, gathering into cumulus onlookers, intangible.
I attempt a reversal, close my eyes to concentrate on sending
soothing thoughts to her, in phrases my mother might have used
hush little baby, don't you cry, I picture a mother rocking her.

We share a tender arc later when the daughter smiles at me, from his lap.
I offer tangerine segments, her chubby fingers barely close over two.
Her father gives a thin smile, jiggles her and says "What do you say?
What do you say? What do you say?"
while her eyes grow rounder and her cheeks begin a panicky puffing.
I feel the red piercing again. I hate him and know it's wrong. I cut in,
"You're welcome, sweetie." I say nothing to him. Again the dagger,
the unzipped violence, the murderous interior, even my syrupy words
are an act of aggression against him, a way to say "*You* shut up, you bastard."
Measured violence against violence, steps in a blind direction.

She will love him, he will love her and still this pairing could go badly.
While inside me flashes of compassion and rage continue their clash and clang.
My enemy self seems stronger than the will to love. Anger asserts itself
in knifeblade turns. Is "to lead" the same as "to dominate"?
This twist of back and forth—the water of welcome, the burned village,
Samaritan, rapist, prayer, taunt, promise, bribe, embrace, crush
the shared smile and the stoning in the desert
and all the fainting in between.
What peace can there be when even a single crosshatched body
cannot cease its struggle, cannot be free.

Drunk Driving

I love the feel of it, the rush
of warm air through the window, pleasant
muddle of past and present, buttercup chain
yellowing my brain, senses both
sharpened and softened, pointillist haze.
Houses fly past on this undulating ribbon
of country road, a woman bending over a rose bush,
a dog lying near a ditch,
swath of orange sky beginning to bruise,
green onion second followed by loamy earth scent.
I glance at my hands on the steering wheel,
the turn of fortune possible with a touch,
minute measurements flow into the soft curves
of this rural route.
Turn up the radio for a sad song.
Croon along, make up a new lyric or two.
Talk to the pine trees winking by
about why you won't go home tonight,
or maybe ever.
Let wistfulness take root,
rue the day.

Bifocals

First, blurred words emerge, fine-print genesis,
strong-boned, jawing air, a sharp contrast from chaos.

Look up and faces across the room take shape,
defined by lines and shadow, a chiaroscuro relief.

Bold exposures. Things, not just the idea of them.
Concrete constructions that I name as if new to the world.

Later, the frames in the mirror return an old uncertainty,
the way my mother's hands attached to my wrists do.

I angle toward the side-long view, a certain slant not quite
so full of light. Learn what's best fitted for soft focus.

Literary Barbie

Inconceivably well-constructed for silence,
her waist is a delicate bridge,
over a small strait between the epic breasts.
The twin sonnet of thighs
taper into diminutive feet,
tip-toed iambs.
Unable to ever bear or pull her weight,
impossibly voluptuous plastic,
perfectly arched pigmentation of eye and brow
nuanced as a wink of ink on page,
like the un-uttered body of words
too beautiful altogether.

That Way

I'm at work when my father,
dead for over a decade,
calls my cell phone and says in somber tones,
Your father died this morning. Come home.

My co-workers are busy, not listening
as I try to explain my early departure.
I need to stop and pick up bread, too,
mourners must be fed.

In the Sac-n-Save the lines are long and confusing.
I start to cry in self-pity and frustration.
A checker looks hard at me and I whisper,
My father is dead.

She allows me to come forward to buy the bread.
She is angelically understanding.
She says in a rose petal voice,
It's always that way.

I leave with some bread and a mantra,
but once out the door, I'm lost again.
I say, *It's always that way,*
but the words have shifted directions.

Instead of breezing southward
the words are evaporating at the edges
condensing, and drifting upward like smoke.
Home isn't where I left it.

I gnaw the edges of my bread, hungry.
I'm probably late by now and I'll need more bread.
Then I remember it's already happened.
The hunger, the bread, the death.

Walking becomes ritual.
I tap my cell back into service and say,
in something like lullaby, *Hush, father. Sleep now.*
I'll call in the morning.

II

Walk out of any doorway, feel your way, feel your way...
Robert Hunter, *Box of Rain*

One Way

My first stretch along the coast
led me away from Dixie strains.
I raise my glass to me and toast

myself for these small gains:
a phrase in French, one solid silver ring,
a sealed canister with Blue's remains.

I took only what I could bring
in the quilted bag I carry on my back,
but I don't need much of anything

now that I'm no longer on the rack
you cranked into almost every day.
I've escaped. I'm on a different track.

You must have known I wouldn't stay,
your spring promise always bound to fall.
Such cyclical waste left nothing else to say.

I emptied out my pockets, one way to Montreal.
So—Farewell, so long, au revoir, adieu.
Don't wait for me to call.

Shame

I can't recall what word or slight enraged me
at recess when I grabbed your boney wrist
and swung you round like a rag doll,
then thud and whimper as you hit the ground.

Got his ass kicked by a girl!
It was a jeer no bully could resist.

Predatory boys gave you swirlies in the bathroom.
In the lunch line they'd yell in your face
Hey, Chester [fingers stabbing your chest]
glad to see you back [slapping *homo* on your back]
as you struggled not to fall.

Your delicate mother, milk-faced and nervous,
brought cupcakes for everyone on your birthday.
How could she have known
how much worse that bribe made your days?
Mama's boy, they hissed on the playground, *pussy.*

That last time you came back from bathroom break,
hair dripping on your button down shirt,
near-hysterical, crying, hiccoughing so hard,
the teacher had to take you outside to calm you.

The boys snorted and laughed,
then looked at their shoes, fidgeted,
squirmed in their seats like small animals
caught in traps.

Tadpole Lament

We scooped up the sperm shaped swimmers in mason jars,
water carefully collected from the puddle of their beginning,
the murky home they knew before the glass womb
with a carefully punctured tin lid to allow them air.

We put gnats, slivers of grass and weeds into their new home,
never knowing for sure what tadpoles ate.
We kept careful watch throughout the waking hours to see
the miracle of transformation that would turn them into frogs.

But they always died overnight out on the porch steps.
In morning light we'd find them changed to floating black commas,
not even a nubbin of a webbed foot visible, no greenish tinge of promise,
nothing that would live or leap from here.

We tried to be good parents, to provide a good home,
to feed them what they needed, to monitor their metamorphosis,
to create a place that they could spring from finally, but in the end
we emptied the jar and gave them back to earth.

Skin

for Dr. Kiene

As the doctor is removing a pinch of my cheek
he remembers a favorite cereal from childhood.
My eyes are closed. I want to see nothing here—
not the needle, not even the gentle nurse.
His voice flows over me, the milk and honey of nostalgia:
They were shaped like tiny flying saucers...
I think "you don't know what you've got til it's gone"
lyric of the beach days when salt and sun whitened my hair,
turned my skin so brown, so brown but I wanted it darker still—
deeper than Coppertone. I feel a little dull pressure
denting my cheek, near the laugh line.
...the same company that now makes Captain Crunch
the milk of human kindness flowing from memory.
When he stitches me up, I feel the tug—
a fish pulled from the Atlantic's blue envelope,
a small note on the bleached boards of the pier,
swaying pylons frothed with sea foam,
sand fiddlers scurrying for cover at every receding wave.
I have a bucket full of them until it's time for castle making,
then they're as free as the fish thrown back.
I open my eyes when he finishes. Ten stitches,
the number of perfection on a less perfect than ever face.
I see the doctor's eyes are dark cocoa and maybe I stare too long.
Now that the lull of listening is over
I want to nibble his fingertips, taste to see
whether they're salty or slightly sweetened,
wind whipped wild sea oats or Quisp and Quake,
the tang of shored up yesterdays buried in the flesh.

Figures in a Field

We sloshed along in galoshes,
through the puddled corduroy of muddy fields,
spattering the air with a feral yowling

or maybe we were singing.

Say we never can go back,
say we just float Chagall-like
in the uncertainty of now,
that doesn't mean the sky didn't eat
the green fields whole
where we lived as children.

That doesn't mean we weren't
then exactly who we were.

After School Lessons

Mother left me at Beulah's when she started back at work,
a silent neighbor if you don't count the endless snap of chewing gum.
She taught me to sort clothes properly and get the most out of every
clothes pin by doubling edges and chicken necks shouldn't
be thrown away and dust everything from the top down and newspaper
with vinegar water was best for cleaning windows.

Her husband was even quieter but kept stacks of nudie magazines
under their double bed that I sometimes made up with
cotton sheets so thin you could see through them. I played
checkers with him after supper when Mother was late getting home.
Instead of 'king me' I'd yell 'Queen Me!' because I liked the
snorty sort of laugh that would break from him and the way it felt between us
that he knew I had gone through his magazines,
not even bothering to put them back the way I found them.

Living Near Lucky

Marisella taught me Cuban obscenities
to fire at winter's stony pall.
While mouthing all the empty words
I was paid to say, I cursed
the insufferable banality
with a profane hybrid
coño tu madre, motherfuckers.

Living close to Lucky became a bonus.
The front page stories, a perverse pleasure.
We tacked them to our cubicles
Lucky Stores Deal with Salmonella Outbreak
Lucky Humane Society Loses Funding
and my favorite:
Lucky Woman Dies in Car Crash.
We imagined a suicidal copyeditor
at the *Lucky Times.*

On those oyster blade days
laughter was as biting
as the steel teeth of November.
Collecting headlines
seemed a better use of time
than naming the grays of pigeon shit
and snow, another crying jag,
or grading freshman essays
for the TA position
that had become a grim prediction.

Receptionist at the Family Planning Clinic

Maria's second week on the job,
she's still curious about the patients,
especially the five here for abortions.
She considers herself compassionate,
but can't understand how
this could still happen in this day…
five seems so many.
Maria never misses a pill or a period.

She surveys them through the open plexi partition.
The oldest is Maria's mother's age,
her hair an orangey cloud from bad dye jobs.
Maria thinks she should know better,
both the hair and the pregnancy,
as she notes the four live births on her chart.

Maria's mother worries a rosary daily,
can't understand why her daughter
would work in such a place.
She snips stories out of newspapers
about staff gunned down at abortion clinics.

Maria ignores these articles.
She wants to be a nurse one day.
Pre-nursing track at the local JC,
she believes this job will help,
even if she's only a receptionist now.

Maria studies the other ones.
Most are variations on a theme,
wearing hoodies, iPods and earplugs.

Later she will bring cookies and lemonade
to the recovery room,
practice her newly-honed bedside manner—
low tones, a Madonna smile.

At the end of the day,
in the deluge of release paperwork,
she processes the orangey Mrs. Moore,
who asks if she might leave some business cards
in the waiting room.

No. I'm sorry. Maria doesn't know if
there's a policy but this one, this old one,
what can she be thinking?

Mrs. Moore reaches past the plexi
presses the card in Maria's hand.
*One for you, then. In case
you know anyone who might need help.*

On a square of cheap pink stock
her name and number,
a picture of a broom,
below that, in crowded print it reads:
```
20 years housekeeping experience,
reliable and professional,
no job too big or too small,
just call
```

When Mrs. Moore, the housekeeper, leaves,
Maria drops the card in the garbage,
wipes her fingers on her pants.

Maria completes the files for the day,
not looking up as the door whooshes open and closed,
where patients slip out like furtive lovers.

III

*Look into any eyes you find by you—you can see clear to
another day*
Robert Hunter, *Box of Rain*

Persephone's Shade

I grew to love the dark time,
discovered another self in those shadows,
one turned traitor to mother's will.
What I could never say to her, or anyone—
how in his rough embrace I gave up my light,
freely abandoning the stark daylight,
to savor his dark rocking.
The shuttering cries he drew from me
nearly crazed me and I clung to him
because I wanted him never to let go.

I no longer regretted the bright
burst of pomegranate between my teeth
that hunger had driven me to,
foretelling a deeper hunger.
The sweetly acid juice reddened
the cavern of my mouth,
traveled the tunnel of my throat,
toward an interior direction
I hadn't conceived of before.

Sometimes returning to daylight,
to my mother's soft instruction, her pain,
the world of sunrise, apples, larks...
I could barely stand the ache, the urge
to submerge myself in the dark,
fierce world of his eternal need,
the other self his body made of me.

Even now, I don't know
which parting was harder,
more full of death.
To say goodbye to the one
who gave me birth
and showed me the light in the world,

or to the one who showed me
the dark world beneath the surface,
the pulsing interior,
the heart-stopping command of the body.

Spinning Dorothy

Dorothy, and Toto too, rode the sky to a land of Technicolor splendor.
Exchanging Elvira and Aunty Em for musical munchkins looked like perfection.
Kansas was so sepia and flat, why didn't she want to stay in Oz, I wonder.

A scarecrow, a lion, a tin man and Glenda, so many would befriend her
after she squashed an unseen witch (a topsy turvy house is no small weapon)
when Dorothy, and Toto too, rode the sky to that land of Technicolor splendor.

But she promptly set out on a winding yellow road to unblend the blender
that had whirled her into ruby slippers from that unlucky witch she set upon.
Kansas was so sepia and flat, why didn't she want to stay in Oz, I wonder.

If you kill a witch, another will pop up. They're like warts that way; they hinder
little girls with smoke and fire, even poppies, to wipe out all the gains she'd won
after Dorothy, and Toto too, rode the sky to a land of Technicolor splendor.

This witch from the west smoked up the sky calling for Dorothy's surrender
and a silly wizard is no match when flying monkeys swarm, blotting out the sun.
Even so, Kansas was so sepia and flat, why didn't she stay in Oz, I wonder.

And who would guess a simple element, a soothing cup of water could tender
such a result as to end her, the scary hag, her evil and her laughter all undone.
Dorothy, and Toto too, then rode the sky out of the land of Technicolor splendor
to Kansas, so sepia and flat, why didn't she want to stay in Oz, I wonder.

Xantippe Confides in Her Neighbor

"…idols are best when they're made of stone.
A savior's a nuisance to live with at home."
                              --Joan Baez

If you ask me, which he never does, of course,
I'd say there's only one question that truly needs answering
and that's how to take care of your family.
I figure, if you know how to make babies,
then you ought to know how to feed the babies.
His head's all up in the clouds
but the younguns are squarely on earth
and they care more about their bellies than beauty.

But he's off to the agora everyday,
which would be fine if he could make a dime.
No, all his high minded prattle amounts to nothing,
nothing resolved, nothing done, nothing earned.
Still, I wash and mend his tunics, so at least he looks presentable.
I mix so much water in the wine even its joy
is diminished, barely enough oat cakes or honey
for anyone in the household.

Everyday I call after him, my breath wasted as his words:
"Bring back some bread! Charge those gadabouts a fee
if you really want to teach them something!
If nothing else at least pick up a jug of wine on your way home."

Catherine the Great
(Empress of Russia from 1762-1796)

You philosophers who write on patient paper are lucky men.
There is so little risk in your treatises, those hypothetical realms.
While unfortunate empress that I am, I write on living skin.

My script, more bold, tilts truer than your letters of learned
spin.
There is urgent weight in the affairs of the flesh and minds I rule.
You philosophers who write on patient paper are lucky men.

My husband, the would-be Czar, dear Peter, was not so foreign
as I, but made of softer stuff, a man only mice could fear or follow.
While unfortunate empress that I am, I write on living skin.

I have not the ease of syllogisms, maxims, or angels on a pin.
Swift action is my proof that I can rule, and am not by gender ruled.
You philosophers who write on patient paper are lucky men,

Do you think me inhumane to devise the scythe to do him in?
Consider it a surface truth, epidermal amulet, a flag as yet unfurled.
While unfortunate empress that I am, I write on living skin.

I would not subjugate myself to be queen consort, had I been
the helpmate or mother behind the throne, I would die unknown.
You philosophers who write on patient paper are lucky men.

Still, not all passions are sated in the crown and loving is no sin.
I am no alabaster figurine, but flesh and blood that may scorch to touch.
While unfortunate empress that I am, I write on living skin.

With my ruby regiments and my scepter, I move beyond the pen.
The eagle insignias I claim come from what I command and win.
You philosophers who write on patient paper are lucky men.
While I, fortunate empress that I am, write on living skin.

Nancy Drew in the Alzheimer's Ward

She is searching for a clue to unlock simple mysteries.
Whose room is this? Where are my glasses? Can I go home?
The bookshelf holds no clues in its volumes of histories.

She scans for an old clock, a staircase, or hollow oak trees,
Some signal to help her decipher which way to roam.
She is searching for a clue to unlock simple mysteries.

Her fingers ache to sound out the clue of the black keys.
Where is that strange message on parchment or on foam?
The bookshelf holds no clues in its volumes of histories.

Briefly she remembers herself and the name of her disease,
until a bell tolling dispels the light and when she reaches for a comb,
she is searching for a clue to unlock simple mysteries.

She has become a sleuth of self, every day she tries to seize
the words that will shed some light on this impenetrable tome.
The bookshelf holds no clues in its volume of histories.

She fears she has lost the password, the message, the expertise
to decode her own ivory charm. She remains a secret, a phantom.
She is searching for a clue to unlock simple histories.
But the bookshelf holds no clues in its volumes of mysteries.

Prolific

He tells me he has published over 200 poems,
his pen just flies. He seems to be waiting
for a reply as I stare into blank space.

My anxiety escalates, endlessly replicates,
knits its own kudzu on my brain
like drafts of drafts of drafts until
you can't tell there was once a barn or tree.
A pulse of alarm beats as he still stares
at me, like a causality he's driving past.

Whitman I dream of your penumbras,
or something, I seek a clever comeback or quote,
I shift my weight but the only thing I can formulate
is a weak *fuck you* and even that
stays stuck in my throat.

Mrs. Robinson Takes a Night Class

Introduction to Literature sounds promising.
I've always been a reader. I can read the lines and between them too.
I've even written a few lines in my day, or used some, same difference.
Professor Ross, I hope he's well-spoken and not dwarfish or bald.
These desks are ridiculous. They need chairs, sofas would be better.
Silly to discuss literature sitting in these absurd little seats
with their hinged lip of desktop on the right, too awkward for left-handed me.
I hope *Lady Chatterley's Lover* is on the list. It should be, excellent book.

Dr. Ross is a woman? Well that's disappointing.
My god, someone should alert her, shoulder pads are only
for football players. That floral skirt looks like a used dust rag.
But that brooding young man over there is intriguing, even with the slouch.
Well, well, look at this one settling in next to me.
This class just got a hell of a lot better. I hope he's Italian, not Mexican.
There was that incident with our landscaping crew.

Yes, yes dear, we know you're the professor—the Birkenstocks gave it away.
How tedious, not a single D.H. Lawrence novel.
Oops, I'm sorry. Can you reach the pen I dropped? I think it rolled under your desk.
Mmmm it still works. He couldn't help but stare.
They're small, but full and still perfectly in place,
this push up is worth every penny, a lovely little luxury.
Ankles into the aisle, oh I still have it all right.
I can almost feel him pulse towards me,
that sort of hormonal surge you want to feel, that pleasant heat.

It's possible I'm old enough to be his mother. The important thing is
I'm not. In fact, for the purposes of this class, I think I just won't be a mother
at all, or wife. My identity will be of my own design. Like a character in a book.
Oh for god's sake is she still talking? The thing to do is make sure we end up

in the same parking lot—that'll be easy enough.
Salvadore. Good. Lots of openings there. I won't call him Sal.
Sounds girlish shortened. No. I'll say it in a way he won't soon forget.
Salvadore. Every Thursday, Salvadore. Starting tonight.

Blundering Alice

When I use a word it means what I choose, says Humpty, on the wall.
Alice laughs, "There's no use trying. One can't believe impossible things!"
A moral: it all boils down to this—who is to be the master and that is all.

Down, down, down Alice went, where she was very big and very small.
Who hasn't almost drowned in their own tears at the end of apron strings?
When I use a word it means what I choose, says Humpty on the wall.

Mushrooms, tea, tongue twisters, Cheshire grins, tall tales and all enthrall
and leave you vulnerable to homicidal rulers whether queens or kings.
A moral: it all boils down to this—who is to be the master and that is all.

Deciphering the riddles of writing tables, time, or a pig-baby's squall—
it's not easy at all. Curiouser and curiouser, the galumphing jabberings.
When I use a word it means what I choose, says Humpty on the wall.

Warned by the rabble babble to hush, she couldn't just shut up, her downfall.
Punning away, she ducked or flamingoed past executions on blundering wings.
A moral: it all boils down to this—who is to be the master and that is all.

Those who say feed your head should probably consider the royal brawl.
Questioning too many things sets the executioner's ax into full swings.
When I use a word it means what I choose, says Humpty still on the wall.
A moral: it all boils down to this—who is to be the master and that is all.

In a Study of the Meadow
Ezra Pound reconfigured

The apparition of these petals;
crowded faces on a wet, black bough.

Old Maid Shuffle

Winning is never easy when you're stuck with such a crew
as a Fat Lady, Thin Man, Midget Man, Lady Midget and more...
well, what are you to do? Just play the cards that turn up for you.

A winning match is a challenge, even the Master Magician knew
that a Lady Clown matched with a Happy Clown might not score.
Winning is never easy when you're stuck with such a crew!

Cummings' Balloon Man searched far and wee in springtime, it's true,
but for Flying Lady or Lion Tamer? Hard to know which he'd adore.
Well, what are you to do? Just play the cards that turn up for you.

You'd have to be a Jolly Juggler of Agile Acrobats in this erotic zoo
or maybe a Tightrope Walker to make the love match you quest for.
Winning is never easy when you're stuck with such a crew.

Looking for a Strong Man? A Trained Seal or Wild Man might do.
A Laughing Lion might be just the thing for a little soft-core roar.
Well, what are you to do? Just play the cards that turn up for you.

While the Bareback Rider and Dancing Bear create a hullaballo
the Sitting Elephant in the room is the Ring Master and Old Maid of yore.
Winning is never easy when you're with such a crew.
Well, what are you to do? Just play the cards that turn up for you.

Where the Girls Are

good girls go to heaven
bad girls go everywhere [bumper sticker]

Delilah, Scheherazade, Mada Hari, Cleopatra
smoke and still play Hearts
throw the glitter in the kitty
see who comes up queen

Lilith's tripping talking trash
no one ever shuts her up
Siren's singing, Circe swimming
nude and gleaming
treasures wash ashore

Catwoman stalks
Salome walks head held high
Medea and Clytemnestra started a sorority
a home for wayward wives

Istar retreated to the stars
Morgaine chose the sea
Vampirella's out all night
Xena rules the day

Mae West hums a tune
happiness is a warm gun
the guillotine behind her, Marie Antoinette agrees
she takes the cake never learned to share

and ultimate Eve travels with her tales
lugging Pandora's box from town to town
inside is Eden's Jeannie alternating all that's evil
and all that's gone for good

IV

It's just a box of rain, I don't know who put it there
Robert Hunter, *Box of Rain*

This Inside is My House

I tucked myself in and under a blanket of useless angst. I thought an egg
might do me good, if it would cook itself, if it would just do that for me
if then maybe some bread, a new mantra, a darling, some jam too would
appear, appear to me like a tea party from childhood, set out, imagined
and real as real can be when you're a spy walled up in futility and soot.
I'm keeping account of the wall on the clock, crazy hinges perpendicular
to time, that want to separate the inside out, I'm stern with it. Circle back.
Say it three times and grab some salt. Throw it. Behave you monster, you
know the oven's cavernous mouth eats its children and certain poets we
won't name. But I will make some neatness here, in the corners that match
up like flame, I will plank, I will silent, I will not go like that. I will not go.

December's Shift

Snow curls over.
A miniature cornice beside the road
breaks as I walk by,
a wave collapsing into itself,
with a small sound like icy bells shattering.

Whether it signals the end of something
or the beginning
or whether that is the same thing
isn't clear.
The white of my breath
clouds the air in front of me.

A sudden blur suggests a doe
bolting into the cover of trees.
I press the heels of my palms together
until I can feel hard cloven ridges
begin to pound against the cold.

Directions for Early Morning Departures

Before you turn on the light
remember the dream still floating at the surface,
pull the lace end of the sheet up to your cheek and touch,
think *baby* to yourself with no irony or bitterness in the syllables.
Fade back into halfsleep where the dream washes
its foamed wave still curling from childhood.
Recall that song that went with sleep—wind in trees,
or trains or electricity not humming.

Before your feet touch the cold floor
stay warm for just a minute more.
Let your eyelids separate dark from dark,
feel the grizzled nuzzle of your grandfather's cheek,
the cool hand your mother rested on your head.
Turn toward the slight sag, warm hollow, you rolled into
nightly on thin cotton sheets whose rose print
was already too faded to see.

Bottled

So much poured into this fragile bottle,
deceptively small, as if you might hold it in hand
without rupturing the heart.

But be warned, it threatens everything.
Put an X on it and shove the cork in deep.

Opened, it will spill all.
Its flood tides sweep away
rafts of reason
every artifice
every careful structure
everything you have to hang on to.

It won't form the longed for wave to the past
that might signal goodbye
and let you ride on.

No. It will carry you out to sea
and you may never return.

Absinthe laced.
Wormwood on the rocks,
Hemlock ferment
distilled over time.

Lock it away.
Don't even imagine you can swim
its deadly currents.

Quadrille

with apologies to Artaud

There will always be something missing from squares,
like corners with no whores or no streets or shoreless.
Taxis are scarce exactly when you need them, only bugs
bewilder this green dusk which is neither here nor of earth.

OMG WTF the debris rolls through a whirling head this
late and that green isn't fucking absinthe is it? I mean absence,
of course, it's more gin than gem, more thunder than light.
Oh Lord, enough perdition to be LMAO YKWIM TMI.

Tangled up in green spindles that might poke a fairy girl
or boy careless enough to put a hand to wheel but don't you
dare the fabric, the text, the spinning churn of mindless burn
that drew us up in the first place, second set, turn, walk, back.

Here, spider, promenade the tangled web you filament.
You spangle. Deceive with your spinney out of turn.
I see the green through the spaces you have left unwebbed,
naked and discovered souls end different or indifferent stanzas.

Doves and Thieves

Sour hour returned after sweet goodbyes
and truces and angels and flies with no wings.
I couldn't keep the barnacles out of my voice
when I told Templedum *avant vous, le deluge,*
also couldn't help adding *redneck motherfucker.*
It's a word match up made in compound heaven.

It's all up on a wall now where Templedum plays
the town crier spewing numbers and prophesies,
netting packaged breaded fish sticks on dry land.
Whosoever believeth better believeth this,
stinking up the air with his vinegar fries.

The moneychangers are at the gate.
Templedum joins the pack, slapping backs,
slurping cheerwine from slack paper cups,
eating pork sandwiches on stork bread,
crying for the lamb the lamb the lamb.
You dumb motherfucker. You ate him.

This is Outside My House

Fallen branches rake like knuckles across the vole mazes in April earth.
It is not the time of the rose, no hyacinth. Coyotes turn hyena in midair, a trick
of sound we can only pretend not to hear. Here the dappled edges of another
chance plays like light, like the rainbow leading toward a gold that never can.
Becoming is so difficult without a plot. But see here, a fence, an attempt at least.
Order. A sentence. Only everything strains against it when you look at the edges,
sky presses down, earth erodes the stakes, different as teeth grinding, some
incisor, some molar, some fang. The road, then. Sure. It doesn't snap shut,
that's a curve. That's a maybe. An asphalt slurring towards what? Some woods?
A town? An ending? It's wearing out its welcome, drear afternoon of dirt and tar.
Out here, no looking through curtains can soften the bite of almost night air.

Thou still unravished bride of quiet time

Enter the apartment: Hello coffee table, would you mug for me?
No answer.

Ring, phone, ring. It's your job. If not a conversation
        deliver a message at least, a beep, make a peep.

Pillars of books—stand sentries of salt or stone—
guard the place I would lie
my heart
            or head on.

Your dust
plagues me with un—[read, done, said, known]
not lived up to.

Your stories Echo Orpheus, Nightingale, Mockingbird, old men et al
atomic wind tunnel in my yearn urn.

Why won't the music box turn on?

Where is the voice that trembles air?

Whose face is it that doesn't now appear?

My sad covey of gibberish quails in its borrowed or broken vocabulary
        can't sustain the hard swallow, the high C
of the towering father.

He carries it off in his beak
        broken neck and all.

Alas for the unfettered gravity of verses in memoriam
[the throb in cadence slow, the ache of singing each to each]
  They bring me no such peach.

The only small squiggle of suggestion surfaces
from the machinery of this masthead
my spell checker advises:
unravished should be unrevised

Tracing a Distance

A scatter of birds punctuates the field,
verdant between layers of mist at this early hour.
My dog bolts for the small brown birds,
they ripple airward at her approach.

My breath comes out in clouds.
The damp smell of earth and pine
on the chill breeze is home, is here,
and draws a question in the air.
Where is the girl with the rain boots?

The answer may be in the name of those birds—
killdeer? swallow? Their low flight, V wing
never match the photos in any guidebook.
I may have lost my way.

What Light Brings

Dawn sips at the screen
beginning in small bird flutings
champagning the eaves.

The chill air becomes visible.
The dented pillow of crushed feathers,
muffled
down of sleep
down of dreams,

but light rises on sound
what comes in through the window
is a weighted ghost, memory
on a sibilant alphabet
of minor eeeeeeeeeee's.

The pink oval of my mother's rounded nails
small moons of bottom
and quick
then dead.

This is what light brings.

and once my father said
"do you love that boy?"
but it was a taunt, not question.

The gardenia bush by childhood
could make my sister sing
as though to me.
She did this easily
moon in her voice.

Confusion of light
making me want to hold a child again.

Making me again child.

Making me again.

The light gathers density, more heat.
Consonants sheer to the vowels and
become cheeeee cheeee cheeeerrrrpppp
or breeee or wheeeeerripp
The eeeeee's still there but taking on
more hue and insistency.

Mother wraps a sky of blue
always away. Daddy repeats silence.
My sister is corded to a phone.

This relentless day will come.
Birds have prophesied.
The hollow left by my head
is a relic.

The dark folds my fingers make
curling into themselves,
palms deepened into maternal lines,
soft roseate cup,
defenseless
against the invasion of light
the intrusive, uncovered air
throated with birds.

The traitor blackbird
and its kin.

Meadow Grammar

My dog verbs into a god of the verge.
Squirrels object, obscure into brush,
birds burst airward at her imperative voice.

Light is subject to change,
beneath full text trees, tenses shift,
past to present. I am. She is.

The future with its abstract nouns
has no syntax here, active voice abuzz
a nearby bee signals being.

About the Author

June Sylvester Saraceno is author of *Altars of Ordinary Light* (Plain View Press 2007) and the chapbook *Mean Girl Trips* (Pudding House Publications 2006). She earned an MFA in Creative Writing from Bowling Green State University and is currently English Program Chair at Sierra Nevada College, Lake Tahoe where she teaches in the BFA and MFA programs. She is founding editor of the *Sierra Nevada Review*. A recipient of a writing residency at Camac in Marnay-sur-Seine, France and grant awardee from Sierra Arts Foundation, Saraceno lives and writes in Truckee, California. For more information visit www.junesaraceno.com.

CPSIA information can be obtained
at www.ICGtesting.com
Printed in the USA
FFOW05n1727210214

9 781625 490742